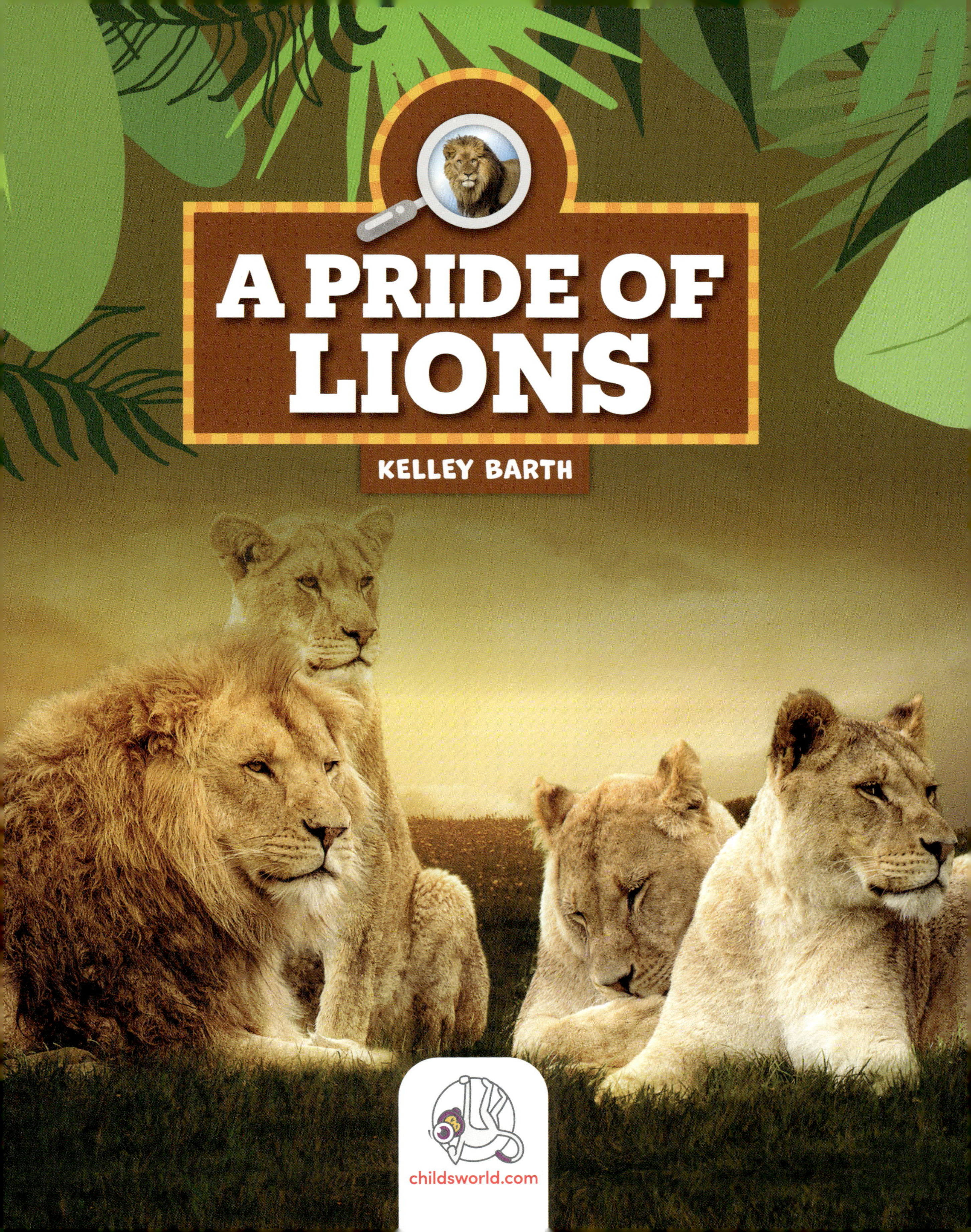
A PRIDE OF LIONS
KELLEY BARTH
childsworld.com

Published by The Child's World®
800-599-READ • www.childsworld.com

Photography Credits
page 1: ©stanzi1 /Getty Images; page 1: ©GlobalP/Getty Images; page 2: ©Anastasiia Verych/Shutterstock;page 9: ©Anup Shah/Getty Images; page 10: ©Kara Capaldo/Getty Images; page 13: ©Stuart Westmorland/Getty Images;page 14: ©Raimund Linke/Getty Images; page 18: ©Gallo Images/Getty Images; page 22: ©krisanapong detraphiphat/Getty Images

ISBN Information
9781503884984 (Reinforced Library Binding)
9781503885868 (Portable Document Format)
9781503886506 (Online Multi-user eBook)
9781503887145 (Electronic Publication)

LCCN 2023937304

Printed in the United States of America

Kelley Barth is a former children's librarian who loves connecting with young people over stories and books. When she isn't busy writing, Kelley enjoys reading, hiking, crafting, and exploring national parks. She lives in Minnesota with her husband and dog.

TABLE OF CONTENTS

CHAPTER 1

Meet the Pride

A warm breeze blows across the **savanna**. A group of zebras feed in the distance. Three African lions hide in the tall grass. They see a small zebra on its own. The lions move closer and the zebras start running. The hunt is on!

There are two types of lions. African lions live on the hot, dry savannas of Africa. They have yellowish-brown fur. Male African lions have big, bushy **manes**. Asiatic lions live in the Sasan Gir National Park, which is a protected area in India. This means no one can hunt the animals that live there. Asiatic lions are smaller with darker manes.

But both kinds of lions have one thing in common—they live together in a group. Lions are the only cats that live in groups. A group of lions is called a pride.

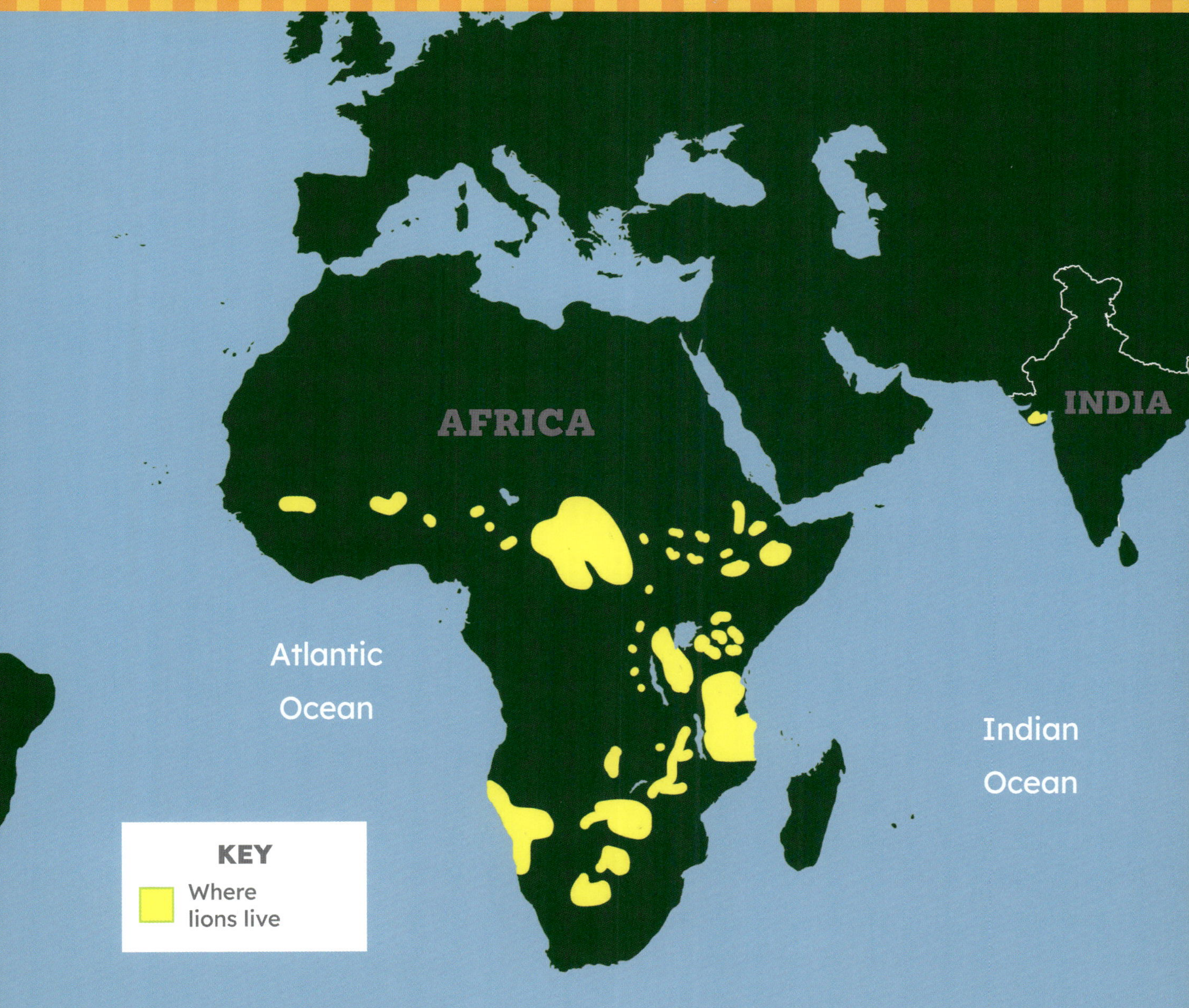
AFRICA
INDIA
Atlantic
Ocean
Indian
Ocean
KEY
Where
lions live

Lion Size Comparison

Male lions are 5.5–8 feet (1–2.5 meters) long and weigh between 331 and 551 pounds (150–250 kilograms). Lionesses are 4.5–6 feet (1.4–1.8 m) long and weigh between 265 and 401 pounds (120–182 kg).

The average house cat is 20-28 inches (51-71 centimeters) long and weighs between 8 and 12 pounds (3.6-5.5 kg).

Lions are very social. Prides usually have two to three male lions. Several females, or lionesses, and many cubs live in a pride. Most prides have around 15 lions. But as many as 40 lions can make up a pride.

Prides are family groups. All of the lionesses in the pride are related. They are either mothers and daughters, aunts and nieces, or sisters. Lions enjoy spending time together. They snuggle, rub heads, and lick one another. Prides sleep, play, and hunt together.

All in the Family

Lionesses usually have between one and four babies at a time. Baby lions are called cubs. Mother lions keep their cubs safe in a **den**. Male lions protect their cubs, but they do not help raise their young. Cubs nurse, or drink milk from their mother, for six months. At two or three months old, they also start to eat meat.

Cubs can leave the den after around eight weeks. But **predators** such as leopards or hyenas often attack lion cubs. Sometimes cubs are killed by male lions trying to take over a pride. Many lion cubs die before they turn two.

Female cubs stay with their pride for life. Males leave when they are between two and four. Some male lions take over a pride by killing the males and any cubs they can find. Some males live together in small groups, and some live alone.

Lion cubs are born blind and helpless. They cannot take care of themselves at first.

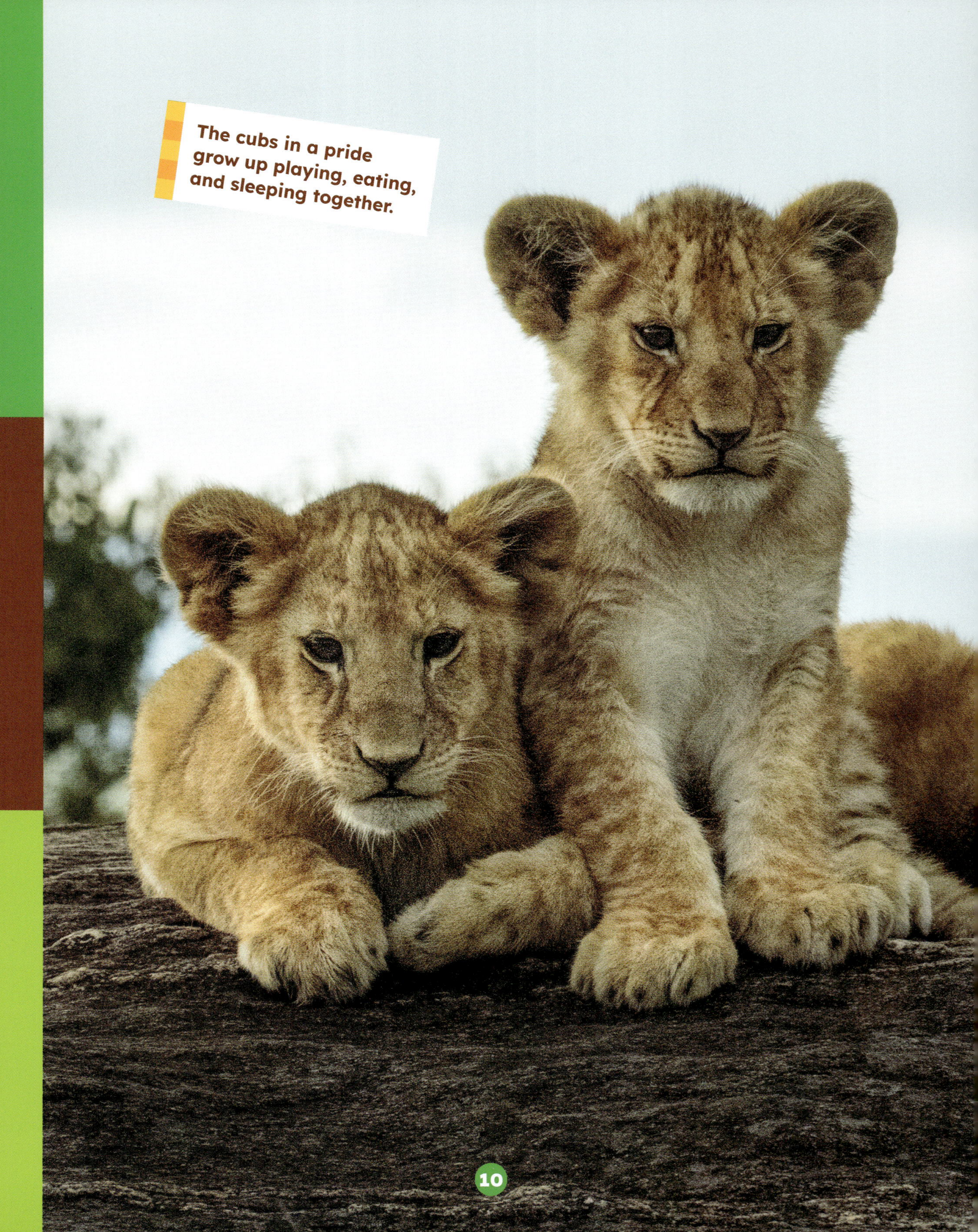

The cubs in a pride grow up playing, eating, and sleeping together.

All of the cubs in a pride are born around the same time. The cubs are raised together. Lion moms help each other out. When a mother lion goes hunting, she sometimes leaves her cubs with a younger lioness or another lion mom. A lioness will even nurse another lion's cubs along with her own.

The cubs nap and play together. They practice pouncing on each other. Cubs practice hunting together, too. These activities help them form a close bond. Older lionesses in the pride help the cubs learn important skills. Cubs watch their mothers and aunts closely so they can learn to hunt and survive.

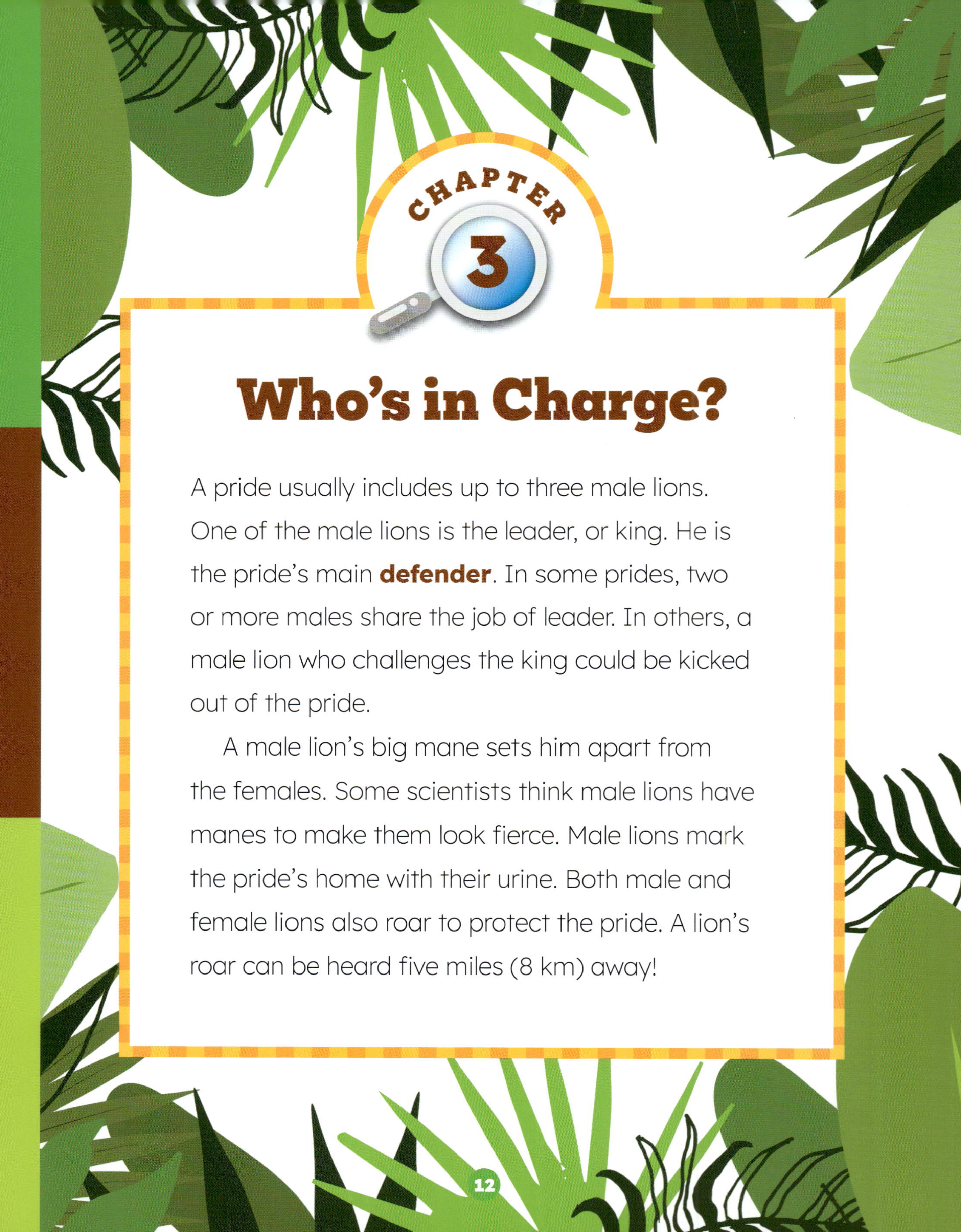

Who's in Charge?

A pride usually includes up to three male lions. One of the male lions is the leader, or king. He is the pride's main **defender**. In some prides, two or more males share the job of leader. In others, a male lion who challenges the king could be kicked out of the pride.

A male lion's big mane sets him apart from the females. Some scientists think male lions have manes to make them look fierce. Male lions mark the pride's home with their urine. Both male and female lions also roar to protect the pride. A lion's roar can be heard five miles (8 km) away!

A male lion's mane is a sign of power and health. Lions with thick, dark manes are usually well-fed and strong.

Lionesses set out on a hunt together, but when a target, they spread out and sneak up on it.

All lions in a pride have important work to do. Male lions protect the pride and **territory**. Lionesses care for cubs and hunt for food. Lionesses are smaller and faster than male lions. Their speed helps them catch **prey**.

Lionesses hunt as a group. A group of lionesses sneak up toward prey. They surround it from all sides. Large, padded feet help lions move quietly. Then, one or more lioness will chase the prey toward the other lionesses. Together, they are strong enough to kill large animals that will provide them with food for days.

LOOKING FOR LUNCH

The pride's lionesses keep the family fed. They are skilled hunters thanks to their excellent senses. They can see six times better in the dark than humans. Lionesses hunt when the sun goes down. They also have good hearing. A lion's ears can turn in all directions. This helps them hear sounds in the distance. Lionesses can hear prey that is more than one mile (1.6 km) away. Good sight and hearing help them keep the rest of the pride fed.

CHAPTER 4

What Makes the Pride Unique?

Lions and other big cats are alike in many ways. They have sharp claws that help them hunt. They are **carnivores** that hunt a variety of animals, some much larger than they are. But every other type of big cat is solitary. That means they live and hunt alone. But lions are unique. A pride of lions works together as a community. They hunt together and raise their cubs together. Similar to a human family, every lion in the pride has a job.

Lionesses hunt many larger animals, including antelope, wildebeests, buffalo, and zebras.

BIG CATS!

There are several large cats in the wild, but only some are considered “big cats.” These include tigers, jaguars, leopards, snow leopards, and lions. Big cats are apex predators, which means no other animal hunts them. They hunt other animals for food and sleep most of the day. Most big cats are solitary. That means they live and hunt alone. Lions are the only big cats that live in a group.

Like housecats that live together, lions in a pride are very affectionate and enjoy cuddling and napping together.

Most big cats, including lions, cannot purr. But a pride of lions often roars together. Even the cubs join in! A pride might roar together to scare off enemies. But sometimes they are just talking to each other.

Prides communicate in other ways, too. They say hello with a hum or a huff. Lions grunt softly to call each other. Lions also use their bodies to communicate. They rub heads and groom each other. Male lions leave their scent on the ground. This tells other lions to stay away. Lions also show off their sharp teeth as a warning.

LONE LIONS

For most lions, prides are a way of life. But one group of lions in Kenya is different—it does not form a pride. Many humans also live in the same area. The lions have learned to **adapt** to their human neighbors. One way they have done this is by living and hunting alone. A single lion can move to a new territory more quickly than a whole group. Lionesses who live here take their cubs along on hunts. They teach their cubs to hunt early. Although a pride helps lions stay safe, some lions have found a different way of life.

Why Prides Matter

There are between 20,000 and 39,000 lions living in the wild. But prides are in trouble. They face many dangers from humans. Prides lose their territories as humans take up more space. Farmers kill lions to keep the cats away from their **livestock**. Some people also hunt lions for their teeth and claws. But killing just one lion hurts the entire pride.

Many people see lions as a **symbol** of strength and courage. Lions also keep their environment balanced and healthy. It is important for humans to work together to help save lions, just as lions work together to help their pride.

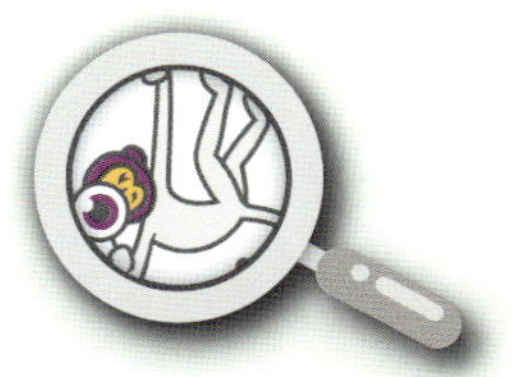

Wonder More

Wondering about New Information

What new information did you learn about lion prides? Write down three new facts that you learned. Did this information surprise you? Why or why not?

Wondering How It Matters

A pride of lions is a family unit. How is a lion pride similar to a human family? How is it different?

Wondering Why

There are fewer lions alive today than ever before. Prides face many dangers from humans. What can you do to help protect lions?

Ways to Keep Wondering

After reading this book, what questions do you have about prides? What can you do to learn more about them?

Royal Lion Crowns

What You Need:

- Paper
- Tape
- Scissors
- Art supplies (markers, crayons, colored pencils, etc.)

Steps to Take:

1. Cut out long, straight strips from two sheets of paper. The edge of the paper can be whatever shape you'd like.
2. Tape the ends of each paper together to make one long strip.
3. Decorate your crown with a pride of lions. Don't forget to include lions, lionesses, and cubs. Get creative!
4. Have an adult help fit the decorated strip of paper on your head and tape the remaining two ends together.
5. Wear your lion crown with pride!

Glossary

adapt (uh-DAPT) When an animal adapts, it changes to better fit a situation or environment.

carnivore (KAR-nuh-vor) A carnivore is an animal that eats meat.

defender (dee-FEN-dur) A defender protects or drives away danger.

den (DEN) A den is the home of a wild animal.

livestock (LYV-stok) Livestock are farm animals.

mane (MAYN) A mane is the long hair that grows around a lion's neck.

predator (PREH-duh-tuhr) A predator is an animal that hunts other animals for food.

prey (PRAY) Prey are animals that are hunted or eaten by another animal.

savanna (suh-VAN-uh) A savanna is a large grassland with few trees.

symbol (SIM-buhl) A symbol stands for or represents something.

territory (TAYR-uh-tor-ee) Territory is the physical area that an animal or group lives on or defends.

Find Out More

In the Library

Bishop, Nic. *Big Cats.* New York, NY: Scholastic Press, 2019.

Humphrey, Natalie. *Lions and Cubs.* New York, NY: Gareth Stevens, 2021.

Reynolds, Jan. *The Lion Queens of India.* New York, NY: Lee & Low Books, 2020.

Roome, Hugh. *Lions: Kings of the Grasslands.* New York, NY: Children's Press, 2020.

On the Web

Visit our website for links about lion prides:
childsworld.com/links

Note to Parents, Caregivers, Teachers, and Librarians: We routinely verify our Web links to make sure they are safe and active sites. So encourage your readers to check them out!

Index